GOD UNDERSTANDS

Published by

THE BIBLE LEAGUE
South Holland, Illinois 60473, USA
Burlington, Ontario, L7R 3Y8, Canada
Werrington, NSW 2747, Australia
Mt. Albert, New Zealand

Printed in U.S.A.
A100-19

COMFORT

How does God
　　bring comfort
　　　　to a sorrowing heart?

In many ways—
　　through the presence and kindness
　　　　of dear ones and friends,
　　through expressions of love and concern
　　　　from those who share
　　　　　　our sorrow,
　　through words of sympathy
　　　　from those who
　　　　　　really care.

And through His Word!

The Bible contains many
　　comforting truths and promises
　　　　for those who are
　　　　　　in sorrow.

Some of those promises
　　are included
　　　　in this booklet.

Read them for yourself,
　　meditate on them,
　　　　believe them.

Commit your sorrow to the Lord
　　in prayer,
And receive His peace.

THE BIBLE SAYS...

"Do not fear,
for I am with you;
Do not be dismayed,
for I am your God.
I will strengthen you
and help you,
I will uphold you
with my righteous right hand."
Isaiah 41:10

"When you pass through the waters,
I will be with you;
And when you pass through the rivers,
they will not sweep
over you.
When you walk through the fire,
you will not be
burned . . .
For I am the Lord,
your God."
Isaiah 43:2, 3a

The Lord will be
your everlasting light,
And your days of sorrow
will end.
Isaiah 60:20b

ACCEPTANCE

It is not always easy
    to accept the death
        of someone we love.

If the death is sudden
    or unexpected,
We are usually shocked
    or stunned.

Even when death
    is expected,
It is often hard
    to believe at first
That our friend or loved one
    is permanently gone.
Death is so awesome,
    so final.

The death of someone we know
    speaks also to us
        of our own
            coming death.

We may be young or old,
    but we know that
    death is no respecter
        of either person
            or of age.

Death is a fact
    of life
That we must humbly learn
    to accept.

THE BIBLE SAYS...

There is a time
for everything . . .
A time to be born
and a time
to die.

Ecclesiastes 3:1, 2a

Man's days are determined;
You have decreed
the number
of his months
And have set limits
he cannot exceed.

Job 14:5

The Lord gave
and the Lord
has taken away;
May the name
of the Lord
be praised.

Job 1:21b

Show me, O Lord,
my life's end
and the number
of my days;
Let me know
how fleeting
is my life.

Psalm 39:4

FEELINGS

How are we supposed to feel
when death takes
a loved one away?

Should we be overwhelmed
with sorrow and grief?
Or should we be filled with joy
because our loved one
has been taken home?

It simply is not possible
to tell someone else
How he should feel
at the time
of a loved one's death.

Feelings simply come—
and feelings will sometimes change
from one moment
to the next.

Do not be overly concerned
about how you are
supposed to feel.
Rather, learn to commit all
your feelings to the Lord.
Be grateful for the times
when you feel good.
And when sorrow starts to
overwhelm you,
Remember that God understands
and cares.

THE BIBLE SAYS...

I cried out to God
for help;
I cried out to God
to hear me.
When I was in distress,
I sought the Lord;
At night I stretched out
untiring hands
And my soul
refused to be
comforted.

Psalm 77:1, 2

O God,
you are my God,
Earnestly I seek you;
My soul thirsts for you,
my body longs for you,
In a dry and weary land
where there is no water.

Psalm 63:1

The righteous cry out,
and the Lord hears them;
He delivers them
from all their troubles.
The Lord is close
to the brokenhearted
and saves those
who are crushed in spirit.

Psalm 34:17, 18

Be still
*   before the Lord*
And wait patiently
*   for him.*

Psalm 37:7a

LOSS

When a believer dies,
    he enters directly
        into the presence
            of his Lord.

For the believer, therefore,
    death is truly gain,
        not loss.

But for those of us
    who are left behind,
        the death of a loved one
            is often a heavy loss.

Widows and widowers,
    parents and children,
        brothers and sisters,
            acquaintances and friends
May rejoice at the blessing
    a loved one has gained,
But they are often overwhelmed
    with a sense
        of their own deep loss.
Is it right to concentrate so strongly
    on our own sense of loss?

Perhaps not,
    but God understands
        how deeply we feel.
And He promises to stay
    close beside us
        in our sorrow.
God will never leave us
    alone.

THE BIBLE SAYS...

How I long
 for the months gone by,
 for the days when God
  watched over me.
Oh, for the days
 when I was in my prime,
 when God's intimate friendship
  blessed my house,
 when the Almighty was still with me
  and my children
   were around me.
     Job 29:2, 4, 5

Hear my cry, O God;
 listen to my prayer.
From the ends of the earth
 I call to you,
I call as my heart
 grows faint;
Lead me to the rock
 that is higher
  than I.
     Psalm 61:1, 2

In the day of trouble
 he will keep me safe
  in his dwelling;
He will hide me
 in the shelter
  of his tabernacle
   and set me high
    upon a rock.
     Psalm 27:5

PRESSURE

When a loved one dies,
    there are so many things
        that have to be taken care of.

Funeral arrangements,
    financial matters,
        personal affairs—
Important decisions on all kinds
    of pressing concerns.
Our whole being seems to groan
    under a heavy load
        of pressure.

God understands
    that pressure.

He promises to give you
    wisdom and strength
        equal to your tasks.
He promises that His grace
    will be sufficient
        for you.

Do not try
    to do everything
        in your own strength.

Cast your burdens
    upon the Lord,
And He will surely
    sustain you.

THE BIBLE SAYS...

Cast your cares
on the Lord
and he will sustain you.
He will never let
the righteous fall.

Psalm 55:22

God is our refuge and strength,
an ever present help
in trouble.
Therefore we will not fear,
though the earth give way
and the mountains fall
into the heart of the sea.

Psalm 46:1, 2

"My grace is sufficient
for you,
For my power
is made perfect
in weakness."

II Corinthians 12:9

I can do everything
through him
who gives me strength.

Philippians 4:13

---

*"My grace
    is sufficient
        for you,
For my power
    is made perfect
        in weakness."*

II Corinthians 12:9

ANGER

Sometimes the strongest feeling
    a person has at the time
        of a loved one's death
            is anger.
Is it really possible?
    Can someone who is full
        of sadness and grief
            also be angry?
Can someone who has learned
    to trust the Lord
        still be angry?
Yes, sometimes.
    Angry at God
        for taking your loved one
            away from you.
Angry at doctors
    for not keeping your loved one alive.
Angry at others
    who talk so lightly about comfort
        when they have never gone
            through sorrow themselves.
Angry at yourself
    for not showing more love
        while you had the opportunity.
Let go of your anger!
Commit your anger
    to the Lord.
Ask Him to take away
    the bitterness of your heart.
Ask Him to fill your heart
    with peace.

THE BIBLE SAYS...

Do not let the sun go down
while you are still angry,
And do not give
the devil
a foothold.

Ephesians 4:26b, 27

In your anger
do not sin;
When you are on your beds,
search your hearts
and be silent.

Psalm 4:4

When my heart was grieved
and my spirit embittered,
I was senseless
and ignorant . . . .
Yet I am always with you;
you hold me
by my right hand.

Psalm 73:21-23

Though you have made me see
troubles, many and bitter,
You will restore
my life again;
From the depths of the earth
you will again
bring me up.

Psalm 71:20

GUILT

When we stop to consider
    what we might have done
      for our loved ones,
We are often burdened
    with a sense of
      guilt.

There may be many things
    we wish we could do over.
There may have been kind words
    we wanted to say,
Or kind deeds
    we wanted to do,
But we always put them off.

There may have been amends
    we intended to make
Or things we wanted to set right,
    but we never did.
And now it is too late.

And so the feelings of guilt
    add to the sorrow and loss
      that we already feel.

Does God understand these feelings, too?
    Of course He does!

And where we have really failed,
    God will graciously forgive us
      if we humbly ask Him to.

And then, after we have been forgiven,
    let us begin to speak and live and love
      as we wish we had done before.

THE BIBLE SAYS...

Turn to me
  and be gracious to me,
For I am lowly
  and afflicted.
The troubles of my heart
  have multiplied;
Free me from my anguish.

Look upon my affliction
  and my distress
And take away
  all my sins.

                    Psalm 25:16-18

The Lord is compassionate and gracious,
  slow to anger,
    abounding in love.
He will not always accuse,
  nor will he harbor his anger forever;
He does not treat us
  as our sins deserve
    or repay us
      according to our iniquities.
For as high as the heavens are
  above the earth,
So great is his love
  for those who
    fear him;
As far as the east is from the west,
  so far has he removed
    our transgressions
      from us.

                    Psalm 103:8-12

JOY

There are times
> *when the death of a loved one*
>> *comes as an answer to prayer.*

Sometimes people suffer greatly
> *from an incurable disease.*

Others lose completely
> *all desire to live,*

Because there seems
> *so very little*
>> *to live for.*

They may have often prayed
> *that God would*
>> *end their suffering and*
>>> *take them home.*

When such a person dies,
> *there is reason for great joy.*

There may still be tears
> *along with the joy,*

And there may be a sense of loss
> *along with the gratitude,*

But the fundamental feeling
> *is one of*
>> *deep joy.*

A dear and precious loved one
> *has been welcomed*
>> *into the very presence*
>>> *of God.*

THE BIBLE SAYS...

"Blessed are the dead
who die in the Lord . . . .
They will rest
from their labor,
For their deeds
will follow them."

Revelation 14:13

For to me
to live is Christ
and to die is gain.

Philippians 1:21

Therefore, they are before the throne
of God
And serve him day and night
in his temple . . . .
Never again will they hunger;
never again will they thirst . . . .
For the Lamb at the center of the throne
will be their shepherd;
He will lead them
to springs of living water,
And God will wipe away
every tear
from their eyes.

Revelation 7:15-17

Those who hope in the Lord
will renew their strength.
They will soar on wings
like eagles;
They will run
and not grow weary,
They will walk
and not be faint.

Isaiah 40:31

SOLITUDE

Visitors and friends
    are very important to you
        in your time
           of sorrow.
But it is also very important for you
    to spend some time
        alone.

When you are alone
    you can pour out your inmost feelings
        to your Father in heaven.
You can let go the feelings
    that you did not
        dare or care
           to express in public.

God understands
    far better than anyone else
        exactly how you feel.
God is also more patient,
    more loving and
        more kind than others.
And He will respond
    in mercy and in love
To the deepest feelings
    of your heart.

THE BIBLE SAYS...

Jesus said,
"Come with me by yourselves
to a quiet place
and get some rest."
Mark 6:31b

On my bed I remember you;
I think of you
through the watches of the night.
I stay close to you;
your right hand
upholds me.
Psalm 63:6, 8

I will praise the Lord
who counsels me;
Even at night
my heart instructs me.
I have set the Lord always before me.
Because he is at my right hand,
I will not be shaken.
Psalm 16:7, 8

LONELINESS

No one really understands
    what loneliness is
Until he has experienced it
    himself.

Widows and widowers
    know what it means
        to be lonely.
Those who have lost their dearest friend
    or a constant companion
        or a precious child
Know what it means
    to be lonely.

An empty chair,
    a quiet house,
        silent meals,
            and long dark nights—
All these intensify
    the awesome feelings
        of loneliness.

Those who have never experienced
    true loneliness
May say they understand,
    but they really don't.

But God understands.
    God understands completely.
And God promises to go with you
    through the long dark valley
        of your present loneliness.

You may still often _feel_ lonely,
    but you will never be alone.

THE BIBLE SAYS...

The Lord himself
goes before you
and will be with you;
He will never leave you
nor forsake you.
Do not be afraid;
do not be discouraged.

Deuteronomy 31:8

The Lord is my shepherd,
I shall lack nothing.
Even though I walk
through the valley
of the shadow
of death,
I will fear no evil,
for you are with me;
Your rod and your staff,
they comfort me.
Surely goodness and love
will follow me
all the days
of my life,
And I will dwell
in the house of the Lord
forever.

Psalm 23:1, 4, 6

TEARS

Tears are often a gift
    of God.
Tears help to relieve
        the tension that has built up
            inside you.

Tears say how deeply you feel
        and how much
            you care.
Tears speak for you
        when you cannot find
            words.
You never have to be ashamed
        of honest tears.

God sees through your tears
        to the pain and sorrow
            of your heart.
Your tears are precious
        to Him.

And some day,
        when earthly life is past,
God will wipe away
        all tears
            from your eyes.
And all suffering
        and pain
            and sorrow
Will forever be done away.

THE BIBLE SAYS...

I am worn out from groaning;
*   all night long I flood my bed*
*   with weeping*
*   and drench my couch*
*   with tears.*

*   Psalm 6:6*

Hear my prayer, O Lord,
*   listen to my cry for help;*
Be not deaf
*   to my weeping.*

*   Psalm 39:12a*

The Lord is good to those
*   whose hope is in him,*
*   to the one who seeks him.*
For he does not willingly
*   bring affliction or grief*
*   to the children of men.*

*   Lamentations 3:25, 33*

Then I saw a new heaven
*   and a new earth,*
For the first heaven and the first earth
*   had passed away.*
He (God) will wipe every tear
*   from their eyes.*
There will be no more death
*   or mourning*
*   or crying,*
*   or pain,*
For the old order of things
*   has passed away.*

*   Revelation 21:1a, 4*

FEAR

After the death of someone
who was very dear to us,
Our hearts are sometimes
filled with fear.

At times it may be hard to say
just what it is
we are afraid of,
But at other times,
we know.

We may be afraid because—
We do not know
what it will be like
to live alone.
We do not know
how all the bills
will now be paid.
We do not know
with whom we can share
in total confidence.
We do not know
who will take care of us
if we no longer
can take care of ourselves.

God understands those fears.

God promises
to listen to our deepest concerns,
to provide for us in our needs,
to stay close to us
when we are afraid.

THE BIBLE SAYS...

The eternal God
*   is your refuge,*
And underneath are
*   the everlasting arms.*
           Deuteronomy 33:27a

And my God
*   will meet all your needs*
According to his glorious riches
*   in Christ Jesus.*
           Philippians 4:19

Are not five sparrows sold
*   for two pennies?*
Yet not one of them is forgotten
*   by God.*
Indeed, the very hairs of your head
*   are all numbered.*
Don't be afraid;
*   you are worth more*
*   than many sparrows.*
           Luke 12:6, 7

Be strong and courageous.
*   Do not be afraid*
*   or terrified . . .*
For the Lord your God
*   goes with you;*
He will never leave you
*   nor forsake you.*
           Deuteronomy 31:6

*Cast all your anxiety
on him
Because he cares
for you.*

I Peter 5:7

QUESTIONS

Amid the swirling thoughts
    that go through your mind
      in a time of sorrow
        are questions.
Hard questions.
Questions that cannot always
    be answered.

Why do the righteous
    suffer and die,
While the wicked
    go on to enjoy their sinful ways?

Why do the aged
    live on and on
      with nothing to do,
While mothers and fathers
    and little children
      are taken away?

Why do some people
    get restored to health,
While others die
    from the same disease—
And both have prayed?

Does God listen
    to our questions?
Does He care
    that we cannot understand?

Of course, He listens.
Of course, He cares.

THE BIBLE SAYS...

"Why is light given
*   to those in misery,*
And life
*   to the bitter of soul,*
*   to those who long for death*
*   that does not come?"*
                    Job 3:20, 21a

"Why do the wicked live on,
*   growing old*
*   and increasing in power?"*
                    Job 21:7

"Does it please you (God)
*   to oppress me*
*   to spurn the work*
*   of your hands,*
While you smile
*   on the schemes*
*   of the wicked?"*
                    Job 10:3

"How long must I wrestle
*   with my thoughts*
And every day
*   have sorrow*
*   in my heart? . . .*
Look on me and answer,
*   O Lord my God."*
                    Psalm 13:2a, 3a

ANSWERS

The Bible never tells us
that all our questions will be answered
and every puzzling problem will be solved
in this life.

But God tells us enough
so that we may be assured
that He has the answers
even when we don't.

God is righteous and holy
and good.
God does what is best
for His children—
always.
He asks us to trust Him
even when we cannot
understand Him.
He asks us to follow Him
even when we cannot clearly see
where He is leading.

God will never leave us
or lead us astray.
His ways will always
lead us safely home.
And, when we are safely home,
then all our puzzling questions
will at last
be answered.
And we, at last,
shall fully understand.

THE BIBLE SAYS...

"As the heavens are higher
than the earth,
So are my ways
higher than your ways
And my thoughts
than your thoughts."
Isaiah 55:9

And we know that in all things
God works for the good
of those who love him,
Who have been called
according to his purpose.
Romans 8:28

O the depth of the riches
of the wisdom and knowledge
of God!
How unsearchable his judgments,
and his paths
beyond tracing out!
Romans 11:33

Now I know in part;
then I shall know fully,
even as I am fully known.
I Corinthians 13:12b

HOME

For many of us,
     home is the most wonderful place
          on the entire earth.
For us home means acceptance,
     understanding, fellowship,
          and love.

But no matter how lovely
     our earthly home,
The time comes
     when we must leave it.
All of us.

And then,
     where
          will
               our
                    home
                         be?

For the Christian who dies,
     home is heaven.
And heaven is happiness
     and glory
          and peace.
To be in heaven
     is to be in the blessed presence
          of God.
To be in heaven
     is to be home!

THE BIBLE SAYS...

Jesus said,
    "Do not let your hearts
      be troubled.
    Trust in God;
      trust also in me.
    In my Father's house
      are many rooms;
    If it were not so,
      I would have told you.
    I am going there
      to prepare a place for you,
    I will come back
      and take you to be with me
    That you also may be
      where I am."
                John 14:1-3

Therefore we are always confident
    and know that
As long as we are at home
    in the body
We are away
    from the Lord.
We live by faith,
    not by sight.
We are confident,
    I say,
And would prefer to be
    away from the body
And at home
    with the Lord.
             II Corinthians 5:6-8

Praise be to the God and Father
of our Lord Jesus Christ!
In his great mercy
he has given us new birth
into a living hope . . .
and
into an inheritance
that can never
perish,
spoil or
fade—
Kept in heaven for you.

I Peter 1:3, 4

GLORY

The Bible does not answer
all our questions
concerning death.

But it makes very clear
that all the sufferings
of this present life
Cannot begin to be compared
with the glory
that awaits the children
of God.

The most glorious earthly scene
that we can imagine
Cannot begin to be compared
with the glory
that is to come.

For the child of God,
death is the gateway
to glory.
That's why the Bible
can speak of
a believer's death
as gain.

Jesus Christ has taken away
the fear of death
And has replaced it with
the hope of glory.

THE BIBLE SAYS...

I consider that our present sufferings
are not worth comparing
with the glory
that will be revealed in us.
Romans 8:18

Therefore we do not
lose heart.
Though outwardly
we are wasting away,
Yet inwardly we are being renewed
day by day.
For our light and momentary troubles
are achieving for us
an eternal glory
that far outweighs them all.
So we fix our eyes
not on what is seen,
But on what
is unseen.
For what is seen
is temporary,
But what is unseen
is eternal.

II Corinthians 4:16-18

VICTORY

Those who believe
in Jesus Christ
Are promised a glorious victory
over the power of death.
However, final victory
does not come
Until the day
of future resurrection.
On that great day,
the dead in Christ shall rise
With bodies full of glory
like the resurrection body
of Christ Himself.
The new bodies of believers
will never become sick
or suffer
or die.
There will be no weakness
or infirmity
or pain.
There will be only
strength and health
With perfect soundness
in every part.
When that time comes,
our victory in Jesus
will be finally complete.
Death will be no more,
and sorrow and sighing
will forever flee
away.

THE BIBLE SAYS...

The Lord Jesus Christ . . .
will transform our lowly bodies
So that they will be like
his glorious body.

Philippians 3:20, 21

The body that is sown is perishable,
it is raised imperishable;
It is sown in dishonor,
it is raised in glory;
It is sown in weakness,
it is raised in power;
It is sown a natural body,
it is raised a spiritual body.
When the perishable has been clothed
with the imperishable,
And the mortal
with immortality,
Then the saying that is written
will come true:
"Death has been swallowed up
in victory."

I Corinthians 15:42b-44, 54

God himself will be with them
and be their God.
He will wipe away every tear
from their eyes.
There will be no more death
or mourning or crying or pain,
For the old order of things
has passed away.

Revelation 21:3, 4

INVITATION

The victory and glory
* described in these pages*
Are promised to everyone
* who trusts in Jesus Christ*
* as Savior and Lord.*

Those who trust in Jesus
* have no fear of death*
And are not afraid
* of the coming judgment.*

If you have not yet
* put your trust in Jesus,*
We invite you
* to do so now*
By praying the following prayer
* or a similar prayer*
* of your own.*

"Dear God,
* Please be merciful to me*
* and take away the guilt*
*   of all my failures and sins.*
* I believe that Jesus died*
* and rose again for me,*
* And in humble trust*
* I now accept from you*
*   the precious gift*
*   of everlasting life.*
* In Jesus' name. Amen."*

The Bible Says...

For God so loved the world
    that he gave
        his one and only Son,
That whoever believes in him
    shall not perish
        but have eternal life.
                John 3:16

Jesus said,
    "I tell you the truth,
        whoever hears my word
           and believes him who sent me
    Has eternal life
        and will not be condemned;
    He has crossed over
        from death to life."
                John 5:24

Dear friends,
    Now we are children
        of God,
    And what we will be
        has not yet been made known.
    But we know
        that when he appears,
    We shall be
        like him,
    For we shall see him
        as he is.
                I John 3:2

This booklet has been given to you by

If you are not already involved
in the worship and fellowship
of a Bible-believing church,
we invite you
to write or call us.
We will be happy to help you.